KETO MEAL PREP COOKBOOK FOR BEGINNERS

1000 Days Of Delicious Low-Carb, High-Fat Recipes With 8 Weekly Ketogenic Plans Including Intermittent Fasting And Carb-Up Meal Plans| Full Color Version

GLORIA R. REED

Copyright© 2023 By Gloria R. Reed Rights Reserved

This book is copyright protected. It is only for personal use. You cannot amend, distribute, sell, use, quote or paraphrase any part of the content within this book, without the consent of the author or publisher.

Under no circumstances will any blame or legal responsibility be held against the publisher, or author, for any damages, reparation, or monetary loss due to the information contained within this book, either directly or indirectly.

Disclaimer Notice:

Please note the information contained within this document is for educational and entertainment purposes only. All effort has been executed to present accurate, up to date, reliable, complete information. No warranties of any kind are declared or implied. Readers acknowledge that the author is not engaged in the rendering of legal, financial, medical or professional advice. The content within this book has been derived from various sources. Please consult a licensed professional before attempting any techniques outlined in this book.

By reading this document, the reader agrees that under no circumstances is the author responsible for any losses, direct or indirect, that are incurred as a result of the use of the information contained within this document, including, but not limited to, errors, omissions, or inaccuracies.

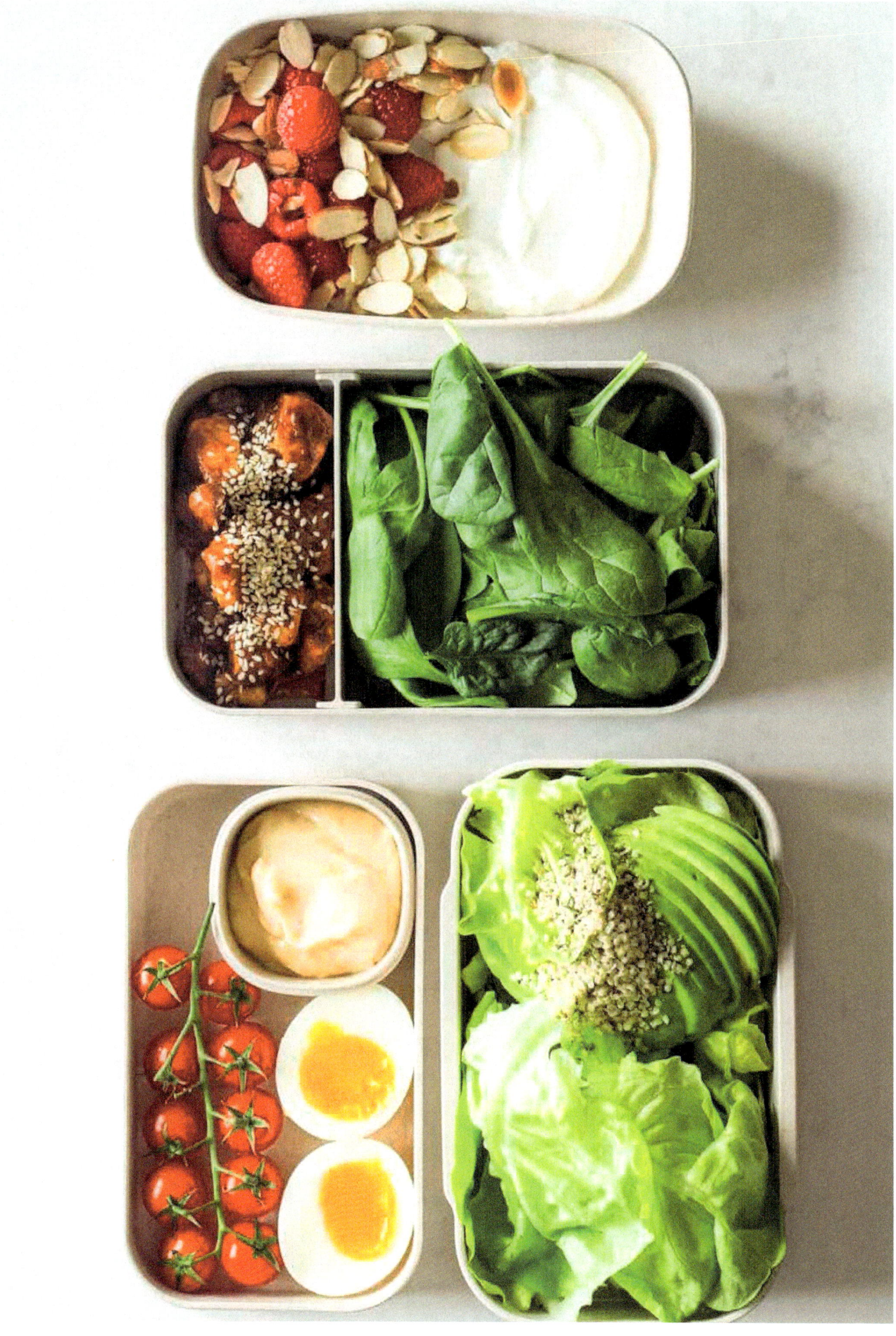

Table of Contents

Introduction	1
Chapter 1	
Basics of Keto Diet	2
How the Keto Diet Works	3
Understanding the Essential Macros	3
Calculating your Personal Macro Requirements	3
Chapter 2	
Start your Keto Diet Journey	5
Meal Prepping for the Keto Diet	6
Choosing Meal Prep Containers	6
Labeling your Containers	7
Meal Prepping Equipment	7
Chapter 3	
8 Weekly Ketogenic Plans	8
Week 1 Fasting Meal Plan	9
Week 2 Post Fasting Meal Plan	10
Week 3 Keto Meal Plan	11
Week 4 Keto Meal Plan	13
Week 5 Keto Meal Plan	15
Week 6 Keto Meal Plan	17
Week 7 Carb-Up Meal Plan	19
Week 8 Carb-Up Meal Plan	21

Chapter 4	
Juices and Herbal Tea Recipes	23
Vanilla Flavoured Coconut Milk Juice	24
Chocolaty Spinach Juice	24
Juicy Chard with Lemony Cabbage	24
Greens Plus Avocado Rich Juice	24
Healthy Nuts and Greens Blended Shake	24
Brewed Coffee Blended with Almond Milk	24
Liver-Kidney Cleansing Tea	25
Mucus Liver Cleansing Tea	25
Immune Boosting Tea	25
Chamomile Tea	25
Respiratory Mucus Cleansing Tea	25
Refreshing Kidney Cleansing Tea	25
Chapter 5	
Breakfast	26
Spinach Eggs	27
Eggs Ramekins	27
Coconut Cream Keto Parfait	28
Parsley Omelet	28
Chia Blackberry Pudding with Stevia	29
French Frittata	29
Bacon Bites	30
Paprika Zucchini Spread	30
Eggs with Olives	31
Rhubarb Compote with Yogurt and Almonds	31
Dill Omelet	32

Classic Eggs with Canadian Bacon	32	Pork and Peppers Mix	57
Grilled Zucchini and Red Onion Salad	33		
Almond and Tomato Salad	33	**Chapter 9**	
Almond Milk Bake	34	**Fish and Seafood**	**58**
Creamy Mushroom Soup	34	Almond Catfish	59
Creamy Peanut Butter Parfait	35	Breaded Fish	59
Fruity Zucchini Salad	35	Steamed Halibut with Thyme and Sesame	59
		Blackened Snapper	59
Chapter 6		Cajun-Seasoned Lemon Salmon	59
Snacks & Appetizers	**36**	Shrimp Salad	59
Coconut Chicken Bites	37	Steamed Dill Cappers Flounder	60
Anchovies and Cheese Fat Bombs	37	Spicy Shrimp–Stuffed Avocados	60
Classic Cocktail Franks	38	Shrimp Caprese Salad	60
Pizza Bites	38	Classic Rosemary Shrimps	60
Easy Everyday Brownies	39	Lime Cod	60
Cucumber Sushi	39	Coco Ginger Curry Cod	61
Turmeric Tempeh	40	Mustard Cod	61
Bacon and Spinach Bowl	40		
Walnut Fat Bombs	41	**Appendix 1 Measurement Conversion Chart**	**62**
Parm Bites	41	**Appendix 2 The Dirty Dozen and Clean Fifteen**	**63**
Chocolate and Peanut Balls	42	**Appendix 3 Index**	**64**
Fried Turkey Breast	42		
Hot Dogs	43		
Pork Rinds	43		
Lettuce Wraps with Ham and Cheese	44		
Deli Turkey and Avocado Roll-Ups	44		

Chapter 7
Chicken and Poultry   **45**
Old-Fashioned Chicken Salad   46
Cinnamon Chicken Wings   46
Marinara Chicken Wings   47
Capocollo-Wrapped Chicken   47
Chicken Quesadilla Melt   48
Sweet Chicken Wings   48
Garlic Duck Skin   49
Paprika Duck   49
Lemon Chicken Tenders   50
Tarragon Chicken Thighs   50
Pepper Cutlets   51
Chicken Wrapped in Bacon   51
Coconut Chicken Tenders   52
Ginger Drumsticks   52
Almond Coconut Chicken Tenders   53
Garlic Butter Roasted Chicken Drumsticks   53

Chapter 8
Beef, Lamb and Pork   **54**
Beef Roll-Up   55
Beef & Potato   55
Mustard Beef Loin   55
Cheese Burgers   55
Onion Beef Bites   55
Mississippi Pork Butt Roast   56
Garlic Butter Italian Sausages   56
Air-Fried Rib Eye Steak   56
Basil Pork   56
Mustard Pork   56
Tomato Rib Eye Steaks   57
Turmeric Pork Loin   57
BBQ Beef   57
Vinegar Pork Chops   57

Introduction

It is yet another opportunity to make new resolutions with the New Year. For many people, that entails planning to lose weight and live healthier lives. Keto was my New Year resolution two years ago; since then, I have kept to it.

One of the most important aspects I have perfected in the past few months is meal prepping. I will discuss some of the tips that have worked for me. Having settled on keto as your New Year's resolution, these meal prep guidelines will help you get to the end of the year.

Why Keto

Keto is more than a diet; it is a lifestyle that can help you lose weight and live a healthier life overall. Keto does not restrict one to eating copious amounts of beef. A complete diet is flavorful, interesting, and enjoyable for the entire family.

With that in mind, keto does need some prep time. At the most basic, you need to know how your kitchen equipment works. To help you win with keto, here are some guides on how to meal prep for keto.

Chop Your Veggies Ahead of Time

While protein takes up most meals, veggies are crucial to any keto diet. While meal prepping, a useful tip is to chop the veggies ahead of time. For instance, kale, a great leafy vegetable, can be chopped up in large quantities ahead of time. You can then store it in batches inside zip-lock bags. When preparing meals, you only need to take out as much as you need and leave the rest in the fridge.

Buy Unripe Avocados

Avocados are a crucial part of any keto diet. However, they are likely to brown if you buy too many. To avoid the issue, buy avocados at different stages of ripeness. This way, you will always have fresh fruit with every keto meal.

Use Different Seasonings for the Chicken

Chicken is great for a keto diet due to its high protein and fat content. However, that does not mean you have to enjoy the same thing daily. Instead, use different seasonings for the chicken. When cooking it in batches, use a simple sauce. When eating it in different meals, use various seasonings like chili powder, sugar-free barbecue sauce, or hot sauce. The goal is to keep things interesting during each meal.

Schedule Takeout

Eating keto does not mean you have to home-cook everything. Today, numerous restaurants offer keto options. Try them occasionally when you have limited time or want to eat takeout.

Keep Batches of Soup in the Freezer

Huge batches of soup are a great way to get through a keto diet. For instance, make meatball soup or broccoli cheddar soup in large batches, and store it in the freezer. You will only need to reheat it when you need it.

Keto meal prepping is not a perfect science. Since keto is still relatively new, there is much room to experiment and discover. Everything will be okay if you keep to the basics of keeping carbs low and getting most of your calories from proteins.

Chapter 1
Basics of Keto Diet

How the Keto Diet Works

The keto diet is a low-carb, high-fat diet that has been shown to help some people lose weight. The goal of the diet is to get your body into a state of ketosis, in which it is burning fat for fuel instead of carbohydrates. When your body is in ketosis, it produces ketones, which are produced from the breakdown of fats in the liver.

To get into ketosis, you need to follow a diet that is high in fat and low in carbohydrates. This means you will need to limit your intake of sugary foods, bread, pasta, and rice, and instead focus on eating foods that are high in healthy fats, such as avocados, nuts, and olive oil. You will also need to consume an adequate amount of protein to support muscle growth and maintenance.

On a ketogenic diet, your macronutrient intake should be as follows:
Fat: 70-80% of your daily caloric intake
Protein: 20-25% of your daily caloric intake
Carbohydrates: 5-10% of your daily caloric intake

This means that you should be getting most of your calories from fat, a moderate amount from protein, and a very small amount from carbohydrates.

It is important to note that the keto diet should not be followed long-term and is not suitable for everyone. It is important to speak with a healthcare professional before starting any new diet or exercise program.

Understanding the Essential Macros

There are three main macronutrients that make up the human diet: carbohydrates, proteins, and fats. On a ketogenic diet, the macronutrient balance is shifted so that the body is getting most of its energy from fats, rather than carbohydrates. This is what helps the body enter a state of ketosis and burn fat for fuel.

Here is a breakdown of the essential macros of a ketogenic diet:

Fat: As I mentioned earlier, fat should make up the majority of your daily caloric intake on a ketogenic diet, typically around 70-80%. This may seem high, but it is important to remember that on a keto diet, fat is being used as the primary source of fuel for the body, rather than carbohydrates.

Protein: Protein should make up 20-25% of your daily caloric intake on a ketogenic diet. It is important to consume an adequate amount of protein to support muscle growth and maintenance. However, it is also important not to overconsume protein, as this can kick you out of ketosis.

Carbohydrates: Carbohydrates should be limited to 5-10% of your daily caloric intake on a ketogenic diet. This means you will need to avoid sugary foods, bread, pasta, and rice, and instead focus on eating low-carb vegetables such as leafy greens, broccoli, and cauliflower.

Calculating your Personal Macro Requirements

There are a few different ways to calculate your personal macro requirements for a ketogenic diet. Here is a simple method you can use as a starting point:

Determine your daily caloric needs: The first step is to determine how many calories you need to consume each day to maintain your current weight. You can use an online calculator or consult with a healthcare professional or registered dietitian to help you determine this number.

Calculate your fat intake: Once you know how many calories you need to consume each day, the next step is to calculate how many of those calories should come from fat. As a general rule, fat should make up around 70-80% of your daily caloric intake on a ketogenic diet. To calculate this, multiply your daily caloric needs by 0.7 (for 70% fat) or 0.8 (for 80% fat). This will give you the number of calories you should be getting from fat each day.

Calculate your protein intake: Protein should make up 20-25% of your daily caloric intake on a ketogenic diet. To calculate this, multiply your daily caloric needs by 0.2 (for 20% protein) or 0.25 (for 25% protein). This will give you the number of calories you should be getting from protein each day.

Calculate your carbohydrate intake: The final step is to calculate how many of your remaining calories should come from carbohydrates. Carbohydrates should be limited to 5-10% of your daily caloric intake on a ketogenic diet. To calculate this, multiply your daily caloric needs by 0.05 (for 5% carbohydrates) or 0.1 (for 10% carbohydrates). This will give you the number of calories you should be getting from carbohydrates each day.

It is important to note that these calculations are just a starting point and your individual macro needs may vary depending on your age, gender, activity level, and other factors. It is always a good idea to speak with a healthcare professional or a registered dietitian before starting any new diet.

WHAT IS NET CARBS AND WHY IS IT IMPORTANT ON A KETO DIET?

On a ketogenic diet, it is important to keep track of your carbohydrate intake, as you are trying to limit your intake of carbs in order to get into ketosis. The term "net carbs" refers to the total number of carbohydrates in a food, minus the number of fiber grams. This is because fiber is a type of carbohydrate that your body cannot digest, so it does not affect your blood sugar levels in the same way as other types of carbs.

For example, if a food has 10 grams of carbohydrates and 3 grams of fiber, its net carbs would be 7 grams (10 grams of carbs - 3 grams of fiber = 7 grams of net carbs).

Tracking net carbs can be useful on a ketogenic diet because it allows you to more accurately gauge the impact of the carbohydrates you are consuming on your blood sugar levels and ketosis. Some people find it helpful to aim for a daily intake of 20-50 grams of net carbs in order to stay in ketosis, but this can vary depending on your individual needs and goals.

Reusability: Consider whether you want containers that are disposable or reusable. Reusable containers are a more environmentally-friendly option, but they may be more expensive upfront.

Labeling your Containers

Labeling your meal prep containers is important for a few reasons:

It helps you stay organized: When you have a lot of containers, it can be easy to get them mixed up or forget what is inside. Labeling your containers can help you stay organized and keep track of what you have prepped.

It helps you plan your meals: When you label your containers with the name of the meal and the date it was prepared, it can be easier to plan your meals for the week. You can quickly see what you have available and what you need to add to your grocery list.

It helps you track your progress: If you are following a specific diet or trying to track your intake of certain nutrients, labeling your containers with the macros or ingredients can be helpful. You can quickly see what you have eaten and track your progress.

Overall, labeling your meal prep containers can be a simple but effective tool to help you stay organized, plan your meals, and track your progress.

Meal Prepping Equipment

Most of the recipes in this book don't require fancy equipment or tools, and it's likely that most of the tools and appliances that you'll need are already in your kitchen. It is, however, important to ensure that you do have the basics on hand so that you don't dive into a prep plan only to find you're missing an important tool. Here's a quick summary of what you should have in your kitchen to ensure maximum meal prep success.

BASIC TOOLS
- 2 kitchen timers
- 2 sharp knives (1 chef's, 1 paring)
- 2-3 cutting boards
- Small, medium, and large mixing bowls
- Large frying pan or skillet
- Medium cast-iron skillet or oven-safe frying pan
- Large pot
- Large sheet pan
- Liquid measuring cups
- Dry measuring cups
- Measuring spoons
- Tongs
- Whisk
- Rubber spatula
- Wooden spoons
- Vegetable spiralizer
- Meat tenderizer or rolling pin
- Cooking thermometer
- Large grater
- Micro planer
- Colander

OTHER
- Parchment paper
- Aluminum foil
- Plastic wrap

BASIC APPLIANCES
- Food processor (not essential, but a serious meal prep time saver)
- Kitchen scale (also not essential, but can be useful for some weighted measurements)
- Immersion blender (very handy for blending emulsions and sauces)
- Stand blender (very useful for blending and grinding ingredients)

Chapter 3
8 Weekly Ketogenic Plans

Week 1 Fasting Meal Plan

Meal Plan	Breakfast	Lunch	Dinner
Day-1	Vanilla Flavoured Coconut Milk Juice	Greens Plus Avocado Rich Juice	Greens Plus Avocado Rich Juice
Day-2	Vanilla Flavoured Coconut Milk Juice	Healthy Nuts and Greens Blended Shake	Healthy Nuts and Greens Blended Shake
Day-3	Chocolaty Spinach Juice	Brewed Coffee Blended with Almond Milk	Brewed Coffee Blended with Almond Milk
Day-4	Chocolaty Spinach Juice	Liver-Kidney Cleansing Tea	Liver-Kidney Cleansing Tea
Day-5	Juicy Chard with Lemony Cabbage	Immune Boosting Tea	Immune Boosting Tea

Week 2 Post Fasting Meal Plan

Meal Plan	Breakfast	Lunch	Dinner
Day-1	Spinach Eggs	Bacon and Spinach Bowl	Old-Fashioned Chicken Salad
Day-2	Spinach Eggs	Bacon and Spinach Bowl	Old-Fashioned Chicken Salad
Day-3	Spinach Eggs	Bacon and Spinach Bowl	Old-Fashioned Chicken Salad
Day-4	Eggs Ramekins	Lettuce Wraps with Ham and Cheese	Lime Cod
Day-5	Eggs Ramekins	Lettuce Wraps with Ham and Cheese	Lime Cod

Week 3 Keto Meal Plan

Meal Plan	Breakfast	Lunch	Dinner	Snack
Day-1	Coconut Cream Keto Parfait	Chicken Wrapped in Bacon	Beef & Potato	Deli Turkey and Avocado Roll-Ups
TOTAL MACROS				
FAT 103.8	CARBS 39.4	PROTEIN 62.8	CALORIES 1542	
Day-2	Coconut Cream Keto Parfait	Chicken Wrapped in Bacon	Beef & Potato	Deli Turkey and Avocado Roll-Ups
TOTAL MACROS				
FAT 103.8	CARBS 39.4	PROTEIN 62.8	CALORIES 1542	
Day-3	Coconut Cream Keto Parfait	Chicken Wrapped in Bacon	Beef & Potato	Deli Turkey and Avocado Roll-Ups
TOTAL MACROS				
FAT 103.8	CARBS 39.4	PROTEIN 62.8	CALORIES 1542	
Day-4	Coconut Cream Keto Parfait	Chicken Wrapped in Bacon	Beef & Potato	Deli Turkey and Avocado Roll-Ups

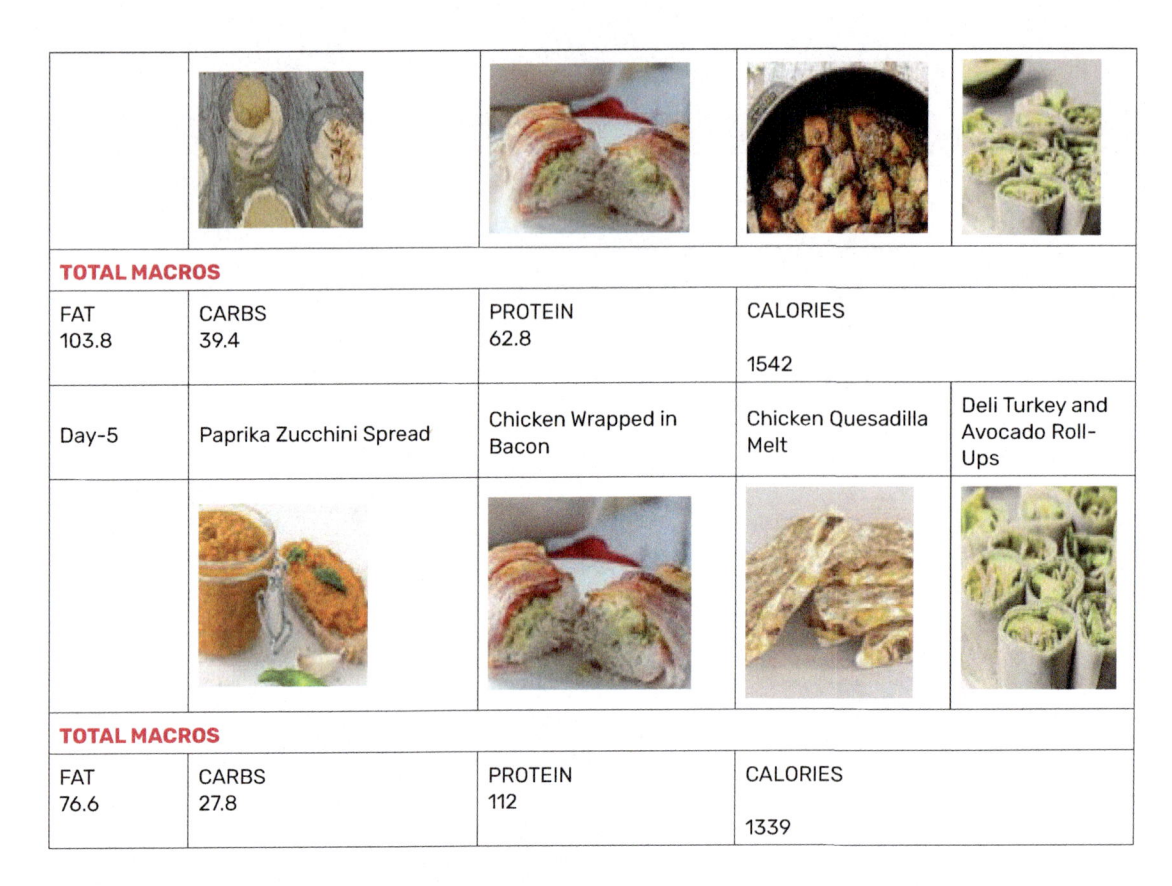

TOTAL MACROS				
FAT 103.8	CARBS 39.4	PROTEIN 62.8	CALORIES 1542	
Day-5	Paprika Zucchini Spread	Chicken Wrapped in Bacon	Chicken Quesadilla Melt	Deli Turkey and Avocado Roll-Ups
TOTAL MACROS				
FAT 76.6	CARBS 27.8	PROTEIN 112	CALORIES 1339	

12 | Keto Meal Prep Cookbook For Beginners

Week 4 Keto Meal Plan

Meal Plan	Breakfast	Lunch	Dinner	Snack
Day-1	Eggs with Olives	Walnut Fat Bombs	Cheese Burgers	Parm Bites
TOTAL MACROS				
FAT 58	CARBS 54.3	PROTEIN 42	CALORIES 865	
Day-2	Eggs with Olives	Walnut Fat Bombs	Cheese Burgers	Parm Bites
TOTAL MACROS				
FAT 58	CARBS 54.3	PROTEIN 42	CALORIES 865	
Day-3	Eggs with Olives	Walnut Fat Bombs	Cheese Burgers	Parm Bites
TOTAL MACROS				
FAT 58	CARBS 54.3	PROTEIN 42	CALORIES 865	
Day-4	Dill Omelet	Shrimp Salad	Cheese Burgers	Parm Bites

TOTAL MACROS				
FAT 51.6	CARBS 29	PROTEIN 40.5	CALORIES 862	
Day-5	Dill Omelet	Shrimp Salad	Cheese Burgers	Parm Bites
TOTAL MACROS				
FAT 51.6	CARBS 29	PROTEIN 40.5	CALORIES 862	

Week 5 Keto Meal Plan

Meal Plan	Breakfast	Lunch	Dinner	Snack
Day-1	Paprika Zucchini Spread	Chicken Quesadilla Melt	Almond Coconut Chicken Tenders	Classic Cocktail Franks (2 servings)
TOTAL MACROS				
FAT 76.4	CARBS 31.2	PROTEIN 107.6	CALORIES 1332	
Day-2	Paprika Zucchini Spread	Chicken Quesadilla Melt	Almond Coconut Chicken Tenders	Classic Cocktail Franks (2 servings)
TOTAL MACROS				
FAT	CARBS	PROTEIN	CALORIES	
Day-3	Paprika Zucchini Spread	Chicken Quesadilla Melt	Almond Coconut Chicken Tenders	Classic Cocktail Franks (2 servings)
TOTAL MACROS				
FAT 76.4	CARBS 31.2	PROTEIN 107.6	CALORIES 1332	
Day-4	Paprika Zucchini Spread	Chicken Quesadilla Melt	Almond Coconut Chicken Tenders	Classic Cocktail Franks (2 servings)

TOTAL MACROS				
FAT 76.4	CARBS 31.2	PROTEIN 107.6	CALORIES 1332	
Day-5	Coconut Cream Keto Parfait	Walnut Fat Bombs	Beef & Potato	Classic Cocktail Franks
TOTAL MACROS				
FAT 106.4	CARBS 55.1	PROTEIN 39.4	CALORIES 1329	

Week 6 Keto Meal Plan

Meal Plan	Breakfast	Lunch	Dinner	Snack
Day-1	Fruity Zucchini Salad	Basil Pork	Coco Ginger Curry Cod	Coconut Chicken Bites (2 servings)
TOTAL MACROS				
FAT 57	CARBS 29.6	PROTEIN 46.6	CALORIES 916	
Day-2	Fruity Zucchini Salad	Basil Pork	Coco Ginger Curry Cod	Coconut Chicken Bites (2 servings)
TOTAL MACROS				
FAT 57	CARBS 29.6	PROTEIN 46.6	CALORIES 916	
Day-3	Fruity Zucchini Salad	Basil Pork	Coco Ginger Curry Cod	Coconut Chicken Bites (2 servings)
TOTAL MACROS				
FAT 57	CARBS 29.6	PROTEIN 46.6	CALORIES 916	
Day-4	Fruity Zucchini Salad	Basil Pork	Coco Ginger Curry Cod	Coconut Chicken Bites (2 servings)

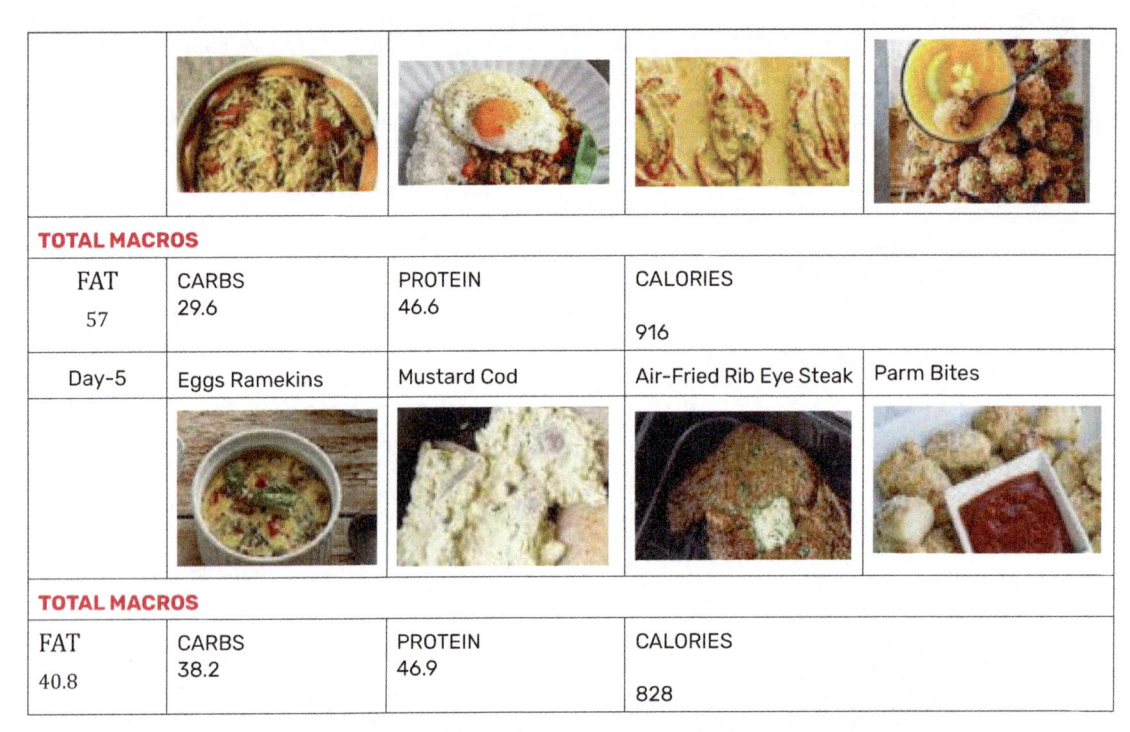

TOTAL MACROS				
FAT 57	CARBS 29.6	PROTEIN 46.6	CALORIES 916	
Day-5	Eggs Ramekins	Mustard Cod	Air-Fried Rib Eye Steak	Parm Bites
TOTAL MACROS				
FAT 40.8	CARBS 38.2	PROTEIN 46.9	CALORIES 828	

Week 7 Carb-Up Meal Plan

Meal Plan	Breakfast	Lunch	Dinner	Snack
Day-1	Parsley Omelet	Beef Roll-Up	Cheese Burgers	Walnut Fat Bombs

TOTAL MACROS

FAT	CARBS	PROTEIN	CALORIES
64.2	54.4	46.3	1084

Meal Plan	Breakfast	Lunch	Dinner	Snack
Day-2	Parsley Omelet	Beef Roll-Up	Cheese Burgers	Walnut Fat Bombs

TOTAL MACROS

FAT	CARBS	PROTEIN	CALORIES
64.2	54.4	46.3	1084

Meal Plan	Breakfast	Lunch	Dinner	Snack
Day-3	Parsley Omelet	Beef Roll-Up	Cheese Burgers	Walnut Fat Bombs

TOTAL MACROS

FAT	CARBS	PROTEIN	CALORIES
64.2	54.4	46.3	1084

Day-4	Parsley Omelet	Beef Roll-Up	Cheese Burgers	Walnut Fat Bombs

TOTAL MACROS

FAT 64.2	CARBS 54.4	PROTEIN 46.3	CALORIES 1084	
Day-5	Eggs with Olives	Walnut Fat Bombs	Cheese Burgers	Parm Bites

TOTAL MACROS

FAT 58	CARBS 54.3	PROTEIN 42	CALORIES 865

Week 8 Carb-Up Meal Plan

Meal Plan	Breakfast	Lunch	Dinner	Snack
Day-1	Creamy Peanut Butter Parfait	Breaded Fish	Air-Fried Rib Eye Steak	Fried Turkey Breast (2 servings)

TOTAL MACROS

FAT	CARBS	PROTEIN	CALORIES
90.5	46	73.6	1608

Day-2	Creamy Peanut Butter Parfait	Breaded Fish	Air-Fried Rib Eye Steak	Fried Turkey Breast (2 servings)

TOTAL MACROS

FAT	CARBS	PROTEIN	CALORIES
90.5	46	73.6	1608

Day-3	Creamy Peanut Butter Parfait	Breaded Fish	Air-Fried Rib Eye Steak	Fried Turkey Breast (2 servings)

TOTAL MACROS

FAT	CARBS	PROTEIN	CALORIES
90.5	46	73.6	1608

Day-4	Creamy Peanut Butter Parfait	Breaded Fish	Air-Fried Rib Eye Steak	Fried Turkey Breast (2 servings)

TOTAL MACROS

FAT	CARBS	PROTEIN	CALORIES
90.5	46	73.6	1608

Day-5	Parsley Omelet	Beef Roll-Up	Cheese Burgers	Walnut Fat Bombs

TOTAL MACROS

FAT	CARBS	PROTEIN	CALORIES
64.2	54.4	46.3	1084

Chapter 4
Juices and Herbal Tea Recipes

Vanilla Flavoured Coconut Milk Juice
Prep time: 5 minutes | Cook time: 0 minutes | Serves 2

- 2 cups coconut milk
- 1 scoop vanilla protein powder
- 5 drops liquid stevia
- 1 teaspoon ground cinnamon
- ½ teaspoon alcohol-free vanilla extract

1. Put the coconut milk, protein powder, stevia, cinnamon, and vanilla in a blender and blend until smooth.
2. Pour into 2 glasses and serve immediately.

PER SERVING

Calories: 492 | fat: 47g | protein: 18g | carbs: 8g | net carbs: 6g | fiber: 2g

Chocolaty Spinach Juice
Prep time: 5 minutes | Cook time: 0 minutes | Serves 1

- 1 cup frozen spinach
- 1 cup unsweetened almond milk
- 2 tablespoons hemp hearts
- 1 tablespoon MCT oil
- 1 scoop chocolate-flavored protein powder

1. Put all the ingredients in a blender and blend until smooth, 30 to 45 seconds.
2. Pour into a glass and serve immediately.

PER SERVING

Calories: 416 | fat: 27g | protein: 35g | carbs: 7g | net carbs: 4g | fiber: 3g

Juicy Chard with Lemony Cabbage
Prep time: 5 minutes | Cook time: 0 minutes | Serves 4

- 4 large Swiss chard leaves
- 2 large carrots
- 1 medium apple
- ¼ small head red cabbage
- 2 tablespoons freshly squeezed lemon juice

1. Peel, cut, deseed, and/or chop the ingredients as needed.
2. Place a container under the juicer's spout.
3. Feed the Swiss chard, carrots, apple, and cabbage through the juicer.
4. Stir the lemon juice into the juice and pour into glasses to serve.

PER SERVING

Calories: 102 | Fat: 25g | Protein: 0g | Carbohydrates: 2g | Sugar: 16mg

Greens Plus Avocado Rich Juice
Prep time: 5 minutes | cook time: 0 minutes | Serves 1

- ½ cup coconut milk
- ¼ avocado fruit
- ½ cup spring mix greens
- 3 tbsps avocado oil
- 1 ½ cups water
- 2 packets Stevia, or as needed

1. Add all ingredients in a blender.
2. Blend until smooth and creamy.
3. Serve and enjoy.

PER SERVING

Calories: 763 | Fat: 77.3g | Carbs: 10.2g | Protein: 3.7g

Healthy Nuts and Greens Blended Shake
Prep time: 5 minutes | cook time: 0 minutes | Serves 1

- ½ cup half and half, liquid
- 1 packet Stevia, or more to taste
- 3 pecan nuts
- 3 macadamia nuts
- 1 cup spring mix salad greens
- 1 ½ cups water
- 3 tablespoons coconut oil

1. Add all ingredients in a blender.
2. Blend until smooth and creamy.
3. Serve and enjoy.

PER SERVING

Calories: 627 | Fat: 65.5g | Carbs: 10.4g | Protein: 6.9g

Brewed Coffee Blended with Almond Milk
Prep time: 5 minutes | cook time: 0 minutes | Serves 1

- 1 cup almond milk
- 2 tbsp cocoa powder
- 2 packet Stevia, or more to taste
- 1 cup brewed coffee, chilled
- 3 tbsps coconut oil

1. Add all ingredients in a blender.
2. Blend until smooth and creamy.
3. Serve and enjoy.

PER SERVING

Calories: 526 | Fat: 50.1g | Carbs: 9.8g | Protein: 13.0g

Liver-Kidney Cleansing Tea
Prep time: 5 minutes | Cook time: 5 minutes| Serves 1

- 1 teaspoon dandelion root powder
- 1 teaspoon burdock root powder
- 1 cup spring water

1. Place all ingredients in a tea kettle.
2. Boil for 10 minutes, remove from heat, cover and leave for an additional 10 minutes.
3. Drain and serve.

Mucus Liver Cleansing Tea
Prep time: 5 minutes | Cook time: 5 minutes| Serves 1

- 1 teaspoon dandelion root powder
- 1 teaspoon Prodigiosa powder
- 1 cup spring water

1. Place all ingredients in a tea kettle.
2. Boil for 10 minutes, remove from heat, cover and leave for an additional 10 minutes.
3. Drain and serve.

Immune Boosting Tea
Prep time: 5 minutes | Cook time: 10 minutes| Serves 1

- 1 teaspoon linden powder
- 1 cup spring water

1. Place all ingredients in a tea kettle.
2. Boil for 5 minutes, remove from heat, cover and leave for an additional 10 minutes.
3. Drain and serve.

Chamomile Tea
Prep time: 5 minutes | Cook time: 10 minutes| Serves 1

- Handful chamomile flowers
- 1 cup spring water

1. Place all ingredients in a tea kettle.
2. Boil for 5 minutes, remove from heat, cover and leave for an additional 10 minutes.
3. Drain and serve.

Respiratory Mucus Cleansing Tea
Prep time: 5 minutes | Cook time: 5 minutes| Serves 1

- 1 teaspoon Guaco herb
- 1 teaspoon Mullein
- 1 cup spring water

1. Place all ingredients in a tea kettle.
2. Boil for 10 minutes, remove from heat, cover and leave for an additional 10 minutes.
3. Drain and serve.

Refreshing Kidney Cleansing Tea
Prep time: 5 minutes | Cook time: 5 minutes| Serves 1

- 1 teaspoon Prodigiosa powder
- 1 teaspoon burdock root powder
- 1 cup spring water

1. Place all ingredients in a tea kettle.
2. Boil for 10 minutes, remove from heat, cover and leave for an additional 10 minutes.
3. Drain and serve.

Chapter 5
Breakfast

Spinach Eggs

Prep time: 8 minutes | Cook time: 20 minutes | Serves 4

- 1 tablespoon avocado oil
- ½ teaspoon chili flakes
- 6 eggs, beaten
- 2 cups spinach, chopped

1. In the mixing bowl, mix chili flakes with eggs and spinach.
2. Then brush the air fryer mold with avocado oil.
3. Pour the egg mixture inside and transfer the mold in the air fryer.
4. Cook the meal at 365F for 20 minutes.

PER SERVING

Calories: 103 | Fat: 7.1g | Fiber: 0.5g | Carbohydrates: 1.3g | Protein: 8.8g

Eggs Ramekins

Prep Time: 5 minutes | Cook Time: 6 minutes | Serves 5

- 5 eggs
- 1 teaspoon coconut oil, melted
- ¼ teaspoon ground black pepper

1. Brush the ramekins with coconut oil and crack the eggs inside. Then sprinkle the eggs with ground black pepper and transfer in the air fryer. Cook the baked eggs for 6 minutes at 355F.

PER SERVING

Calories: 144 | Fat: 8g | Fiber: 4.5g | Carbs: 9.1g | Protein: 8.8g

Coconut Cream Keto Parfait

Prep Time: 5 minutes | Cook Time: 10 minutes | Serves 4

- 4 cups coconut cream
- ¼ cup heavy cream
- ½ cup almonds, slivered
- 16 blueberries

1. In a bowl, mix together the coconut cream and heavy cream.
2. Layer the glass with cream mixture, almonds, and blueberries. Put four blueberries on each glass.
3. Place in the fridge to chill for at least 10 minutes.

PER SERVING
Calories: 618| Fat: 55.9g| Carbs: 11.9g| Protein:8.9g

Parsley Omelet

Prep Time: 5 minutes | Cook Time: 15 minutes | Serves 4

- 4 eggs, whisked
- 1 tablespoon parsley, chopped
- ½ teaspoons cheddar cheese, shredded
- 1 avocado, peeled, pitted and cubed
- Cooking spray

1. In a bowl, mix all the ingredients except the cooking spray and whisk well. Grease a baking pan that fits the Air Fryer with the cooking spray, pour the omelet mix, spread, introduce the pan in the machine and cook at 370 degrees F for 15 minutes.
2. Serve for breakfast.

PER SERVING
Calories: 240 | Fat: 13g | Fiber: 4g | Carbs: 6g | Protein: 9g

Chia Blackberry Pudding with Stevia

Prep Time: 5 minutes | Cook Time: 10 minutes | Serves 3

- 1 cup unsweetened full-fat coconut milk
- 1 teaspoon liquid stevia 1 teaspoon vanilla extract
- ½ cup blackberries, fresh or frozen (no sugar added if frozen)
- ¼ cup chia seeds

1. In a food processor (or blender), process the coconut milk, stevia, and vanilla until the mixture starts to thicken.
2. Add the blackberries, and process until thoroughly mixed and purple. Fold in the chia seeds.
3. Divide the mixture between two small cups with lids, and refrigerate overnight or up to 3 days before serving.

PER SERVING

Calories: 436| Total Fat: 37.9g| Carbs: 22.9g| Net Carbs: 7.9g| Fiber: 14.9g| Protein: 7.9g

French Frittata

Prep time: 10 minutes | Cook time: 18 minutes | Serves 3

- 3 eggs
- 1 tablespoon heavy cream
- 1 teaspoon Herbs de Provence
- 1 teaspoon almond butter, softened
- 2 oz Provolone cheese, grated

1. Crack the eggs in the bowl and add heavy cream.
2. Whisk the liquid with the help of the hand whisker.
3. Then add herbs de Provence and grated cheese.
4. Stir the egg liquid gently. Preheat the air fryer to 365F.
5. Then grease the air fryer basket with almond butter. Pour the egg liquid in the air fryer basket and cook it for 18 minutes.
6. When the frittata is cooked, cool it to the room temperature and then cut into Serves.

PER SERVING

Calories 179 | Fat 14.3g | Fiber 0.5g | Carbs 1.9g | Protein 11.6

Bacon Bites

Prep Time: 10 minutes | Cook Time: 12 minutes | Serves 4

- 10 oz bacon, chopped
- 1 teaspoon dried dill
- 4 teaspoons cream cheese
- 1 teaspoon dried oregano

1. Put the bacon in the air fryer in one layer and bake for 12 minutes at 375F. Shake the bacon from time to time to avoid burning.
2. Then mix bacon with remaining ingredients and make the balls (bites)
3. Now, cook the shallots and garlic in the bacon fat until they are tender. Add the remaining ingredients and mix to combine well.
4. Pour the batter into muffin cups and bake for 13 minutes or until the edges are slightly browned.
5. Allow your muffins to stand for 5 minutes before removing from the tin. Bon appétit!

PER SERVING

Calories: 397 | Fat: 30.8g | Fiber: 0.2g | Carbs: 1.5g | Protein: 26.6g

Paprika Zucchini Spread

Prep Time: 5 minutes | Cook Time: 15 minutes | Serves 4

- 4 zucchinis, roughly chopped
- 1 tablespoon sweet paprika
- Salt and black pepper to the taste
- 1 tablespoon butter, melted

1. Grease a baking pan that fits the Air Fryer with the butter, add all the ingredients, toss, and cook at 360 degrees F for 15 minutes.
2. Transfer to a blender, pulse well, divide into bowls and serve for breakfast.

PER SERVING

Calories: 240 | Fat: 14g | Fiber: 2g | Carbs: 5g | Protein: 11g

Eggs with Olives

Prep Time: 5 minutes | Cook Time: 20 minutes | Serves 4

- 4 eggs, beaten
- 2 Kalamata olives, sliced
- 1 teaspoon avocado oil
- ½ teaspoon ground paprika

1. Brush the air fryer basket with avocado oil and pour the eggs inside.
2. Sprinkle the eggs with ground paprika and top with olives.
3. Bake the meal at 360F for 20 minutes.

PER SERVING

Calories: 68 | Fat: 4.8g | Fiber: 0.2g | Carbs: 0.7g | Protein: 5.6g

Rhubarb Compote with Yogurt and Almonds

Prep Time: 10 minutes | Cook Time: 15 minutes | Serves 4

- 1 cup finely chopped fresh rhubarb
- 1 packet Stevia
- 3 cups plain coconut cream
- ¾ cup sliced almonds, toasted
- Water

1. In a small saucepan, combine the rhubarb, stevia, and water.
2. Bring to a boil and reduce the heat. Allow simmering for 15 until the rhubarb is tender. Stir constantly. Transfer to a bowl to cool slightly.
3. Spoon coconut cream into serving dishes and layer with the rhubarb compote.
4. Sprinkle with almonds on top.

PER SERVING

Calories: 601| Fat: 61.9g| Carbs: 8.9g| Protein:10.9g

Dill Omelet

Prep Time: 10 minutes | Cook Time: 15 minutes | Serves 4

- 8 eggs, beaten
- 1 tablespoon dill, dried
- ¼ cup of coconut milk
- ½ teaspoon coconut oil, melted

1. Mix eggs with dill and coconut milk.
2. Brush the air fryer basket with coconut oil and pour the egg mixture inside.
3. Cook the omelet for 15 minutes at 385F.

PER SERVING

Calories: 167 | Fat: 12.9g | Fiber: 0.4g | Carbs: 2g | Protein: 11.6g

Classic Eggs with Canadian Bacon

Prep time: 5 minutes | Cook time: 10 minutes | Serves 3

- 2 (1-ounce) slices Canadian bacon
- 4 eggs
- 1/4 teaspoon ground black pepper
- Salt, to season
- 8 cherry tomatoes, halves

1. Heat up a nonstick aluminum pan over a medium-high flame. Once hot, fry the bacon until crispy reserve, living the rendered fat in the pan.
2. Turn the heat to medium-low. Crack the eggs into the bacon grease. Cover the pan with a lid and fry the eggs until they are cooked through.
3. Salt and pepper to taste. Serve with the reserved bacon and cherry tomatoes on the side. Enjoy!

PER SERVING

Calories: 326 | Fat: 13.3g | Fiber: 0.7g | Carbohydrates: 5.2g | Protein: 46g

Grilled Zucchini and Red Onion Salad
Prep time: 15 minutes |Cook time: 10 minutes| Serves 4

- 6 zucchini, both green and yellow, cut into ¼-inch-thick slices
- ½ medium red onion, thinly sliced
- ¼ cup olive oil
- Freshly ground black pepper
- 3 tablespoons balsamic vinegar
- 2 tablespoons chopped fresh oregano

1. Preheat a barbecue grill to medium heat.
2. In a medium bowl, toss the zucchini and onion with the olive oil, and season with pepper.
3. Grill the zucchini and onion until lightly charred, turning once, about 4 minutes per side.
4. Transfer the grilled vegetables to a large bowl, and let them cool for about 30 minutes.
5. Toss the grilled vegetables with the balsamic vinegar and the oregano, and serve.

PER SERVING:

Calories: 140; Total fat: 14g; Sodium: 4g; Carbohydrates: 4g; Fiber: 0g

Almond and Tomato Salad
Prep time: 15 minutes| Cook time: 10 minutes| Serves 4

- 1 cup arugula/ rocket
- 7 oz fresh tomatoes, sliced or chopped
- 2 teaspoons olive oil
- 2 cups kale
- 1/2 cup almonds

1. Put oil into your pan and heat it on a medium heat. Add tomatoes into the pan and fry for about 10 minutes. Once cooked, allow it to cool. Combine all salad ingredients in a bowl and serve.

PER SERVING

Calories: 355 Fat 19.1 g Carbohydrate 8.3 g Protein 33 g

Almond Milk Bake

Prep time: 5 minutes | Cook time: 25 minutes | Serves 4

- 2 cups cauliflower, roughly chopped
- 2 ounces Monterey Jack cheese, shredded
- 4 eggs, beaten
- 1 cup organic almond milk
- 1 teaspoon dried oregano

1. In the mixing bowl, mix dried oregano with almond milk and eggs.
2. Pour the liquid in the air fryer basket and add cauliflower and cheese.
3. Close the lid and cook the meal at 350F for 25 minutes.

PER SERVING

Calories 267 | Fat 23.1g | Fiber 2.7g | Carbs 6.7g | Protein 11.4

Creamy Mushroom Soup

Per time: 10 minutes | Cook time: 15 minutes | Serves 6

- 1 lb. mushrooms, sliced
- 1/2 cup heavy cream
- 4 cups chicken broth
- 1 tbsp. sage, chopped
- 1/4 cup butter
- Pepper
- Salt

1. Melt butter in a large pot over medium heat.
2. Add sage and saute for 1 minute. Add mushrooms and cook for 3-5 minutes or until lightly browned. Add broth and stir well and simmer for 5 minutes.
3. Puree the soup using an immersion blender until smooth.
4. Add heavy cream and stir well. Season soup with pepper and salt.
5. Serve hot and enjoy.

PER SERVING:

Calories 145 Fat 12.5 g Carbohydrates 3.6 g Sugar 1.8 g Protein 5.9 g

Creamy Peanut Butter Parfait

Prep time: 5 minutes | Cook time: 10 minutes | Serves 4

- 3 cups heavy cream
- ¼ cup smooth peanut butter
- 1 cup slivered almonds
- 1/4 cup unsalted roasted peanuts, chopped

1. In a bowl, combine the cream and peanut butter until well combined.
2. In a glass, layer the peanut buttercream, almonds, and peanuts in an alternating manner.
3. Put in the fridge to chill for at least 10 minutes to set.

PER SERVING

Calories: 454| Fat: 44.9g| Carbs: 7.9g| Protein:11.9g

Fruity Zucchini Salad

Prep time: 5 minutes | Cook time: 5 minutes |Serves 4

- 400g zucchini
- 1 small onion
- 4 tbsp. olive oil
- 100g pineapple preserve, drained
- Salt, paprika
- thyme

1. Dice the onions and sauté in the oil until translucent.
2. Cut the zucchini into slices and add. Season with salt, paprika, and thyme.
3. Let cool and mix with the cut pineapple.

PER SERVING:

Calories: 150| Protein: 2g| Fat: 10g| Carbohydrates: 10g

Chapter 6
Snacks & Appetizers

Coconut Chicken Bites

Prep time: 5 minutes | Cook time: 20 minutes | Serves 4

- 2 teaspoons garlic powder
- 2 eggs
- Salt and black pepper to the taste
- ¾ cup coconut flakes
- Cooking spray
- 1 pound chicken breasts, skinless, boneless and cubed

1. Put the coconut in a bowl and mix the eggs with garlic powder, salt and pepper in a second one.
2. Dredge the chicken cubes in eggs and then in coconut and arrange them all in your air fryer's basket.
3. Grease with cooking spray, cook at 370 degrees F for 20 minutes.
4. Arrange the chicken bites on a platter and serve as an appetizer.

PER SERVING

Calories: 202 | Fat: 12g | Fiber: 2g | Carbohydrates: 4g | Protein: 7g

Anchovies and Cheese Fat Bombs

Prep Time: 5 minutes | Cook Time: 0 minutes | Serves 2

- 2 (2-ounce) cans anchovies, drained
- 1/3 cup cream cheese, chilled
- 1/3 cup cheddar cheese, shredded
- 1 tablespoon Dijon mustard
- 2 scallions, chopped

1. Mix all of the above ingredients until everything is well incorporated. Shape the mixture into bite-sized balls.
2. Serve well chilled and enjoy!

PER SERVING

Calories: 391 | Fat: 26.6g | Carbs: 3.1g | Protein: 33.8g | Fiber: 0.7g

Classic Cocktail Franks

Prep time: 5 minutes | Cook time: 25 minutes | Serves 10

- 2 tablespoons olive oil
- 18 ounces cocktail franks
- Sea salt and red pepper flakes, to taste
- 2 tablespoons wholegrain mustard

1. Start by preheating your oven to 360 degrees F.
2. Then, brush a baking pan with olive oil.
3. Place the cocktail franks on the baking pan. Sprinkle them with the salt and red pepper| add in the mustard and toss to combine.
4. Bake approximately 12 minutes until they are golden brown.
5. Serve warm and enjoy!

PER SERVING

Calories 155 | Fat 11.9g | Carbs 5g | Protein 9.4g | Fiber 1.4

Pizza Bites

Prep time: 15 minutes | Cook time: 3 minutes | Serves 10

- 10 Mozzarella cheese slices
- 10 pepperoni slices

1. Preheat the air fryer to 400F.
2. Line the air fryer pan with baking paper and put Mozzarella in it in one layer.
3. After this, place the pan in the air fryer basket and cook the cheese for 3 minutes or until it is melted.
4. After this, remove the cheese from the air fryer and cool it to room temperature.
5. Then remove the melted cheese from the baking paper and put the pepperoni slices on it.
6. Fold the cheese in the shape of turnovers.

PER SERVING

Calories: 117 | Fat: 10.4g | Fiber: 0g | Carbohydrates: 0g | Protein: 8.3g

Easy Everyday Brownies

Prep Time: 10 minutes | **Cook Time:** 20 minutes plus cooling time | **Serves 10**

- 1/2 cup butter, melted
- 1 ¼ cups coconut flour
- 1 teaspoon baking powder
- 1/3 cup cocoa powder, unsweetened
- 1 cup Xylitol

1. Mix all ingredients in the order listed above.
2. Scrape the batter into a parchment-lined baking pan.
3. Bake in the preheated oven at 360 degrees F approximately 20 minutes or until a tester comes out clean.
4. Transfer to a cooling rack for 1 hour before slicing and serving. Bon appétit!

PER SERVING

Calories: 123 | Fat: 12.9g | Carbs: 3.1g | Protein: 0.9g | Fiber: 1.7g

Cucumber Sushi

Prep Time: 10 minutes | **Cook Time:** 10 minutes | **Serves 10**

- 10 bacon slices
- 2 tablespoons cream cheese
- 1 cucumber

1. Place the bacon slices in the air fryer in one layer and cook for 10 minutes at 400F.
2. Meanwhile, cut the cucumber into small wedges. When the bacon is cooked, cool it to the room temperature and spread with cream cheese. Then place the cucumber wedges over the cream cheese and roll the bacon into the sushi.

PER SERVING

Calories: 114 | Fat: 8.7g | Fiber: 0.2g | Carbs: 1.4g | Protein: 7.4g

Turmeric Tempeh

Prep Time: 8 minutes | Cook Time: 12 minutes | Serves 4

- 1 teaspoon apple cider vinegar
- 1 tablespoon avocado oil
- ¼ teaspoon ground turmeric
- 6 oz tempeh, chopped

1. Mix avocado oil with apple cider vinegar and ground turmeric.
2. Then sprinkle the tempeh with turmeric mixture and put it in the air fryer basket.
3. Cook the tempeh at 350F for 12 minutes. Shake it after 6 minutes of cooking.

PER SERVING

Calories: 87 | Fat: 5g | Fiber: 0.2g | Carbs: 4.3g | Protein: 7.9g

Bacon and Spinach Bowl

Prep Time: 10 minutes | Cook Time: 6 minutes | Serves 3

- 2 cups spinach, chopped
- 1 oz bacon, chopped
- 1 pecan, chopped
- 1 teaspoon ground black pepper
- 2 oz Mozzarella, shredded

1. Put the bacon in the air fryer basket and cook at 400f for 6 minutes.
2. Then mix the cooked bacon with remaining ingredients.

PER SERVING

Calories: 215 | Fat: 16.1g | Fiber: 1.7g | Carbs: 4g | Protein: 15g

Walnut Fat Bombs

Prep time: 5 minutes | Cook time: 10 minutes | Serves 10

- 2 tablespoons keto chocolate protein powder
- 1/4 cup Erythritol
- 5 ounces butter
- 3 ounces walnut butter
- 10 whole walnuts, halved

1. In a sauté pan, melt the butter, protein powder, and Erythritol over a low flame| stir until smooth and well mixed.
2. Spoon the mixture into a piping bag and pipe into mini cupcake liners. Add the walnut halves to each mini cupcake.
3. Place in your refrigerator for at least 2 hours. Bon appétit!

PER SERVING

Calories: 260 | Fat: 26.4g | Fiber: 1.6g | Carbohydrates: 26.4g | Protein: 4.8g

Parm Bites

Prep Time: 10 minutes | Cook Time: 10 minutes | Serves 5

- 2 medium eggplants, trimmed, sliced
- 4 oz Parmesan, grated
- 1 teaspoon coconut oil, melted

1. Grease the air fryer basket with coconut oil.
2. Then put the sliced eggplants in the air fryer basket in one layer.
3. Top them with Parmesan and cook the meal at 390F for 10 minutes

PER SERVING

Calories: 136 | Fat: 6.2g | Fiber: 7.7g | Carbs: 13.7g | Protein: 9.4g

Chocolate and Peanut Balls

Prep Time: 10 minutes | **Cook Time:** 10 minutes plus freezing time | **Serves 6**

- 1/2 cup coconut oil
- 1/2 cup peanut butter, no sugar added
- 1/4 cup cocoa powder, unsweetened
- 1/4 cup Xylitol
- 4 tablespoons roasted peanuts, ground

1. Microwave the coconut oil until melted; add in the peanut butter and stir until well combined.
2. Add the cocoa powder and Xylitol to the batter. Transfer to your freezer for about 1 hour.
3. Shape the batter into bite-sized balls and roll them over the ground peanuts. Bon appétit!

PER SERVING

Calories: 328 | Fat: 32.6g | Carbs: 7.7g | Protein: 6.9g | Fiber: 2.7g

Fried Turkey Breast

Prep time: 5 minutes | **Cook time:** 30 minutes | **Serves 5**

- 7 lbs. turkey breast, skinless and boneless
- 2 tablespoons olive oil
- ½ teaspoon cumin, dried
- Salt and black pepper to taste

1. Rub the whole turkey breast with all seasonings and olive oil.
2. Preheat your air fryer to 340°Fahrenheit and cook the turkey for 15-minutes.
3. Flip the breast over and cook for another 15-minutes.
4. Slice turkey and serve with fresh vegetables.

PER SERVING

Calories: 287 | Total Fat: 11.3g | Carbohydrates: 9.4g | Protein: 15.2g

Hot Dogs

Prep Time: 15 minutes | Cook Time: 5 minutes | Serves 4

- 4 hot dogs
- 1 egg, beaten
- 1/3 cup coconut flour
- ½ teaspoon ground turmeric

1. In the bowl mix up egg, coconut flour, and ground turmeric. Then dip the hot dogs in the mixture. Transfer the hot dogs in the freezer and freeze them for 5 minutes.
2. Meanwhile, preheat the air fryer to 400F. Place the frozen hot dogs in the air fryer basket and cook them for 6 minutes or until they are light brown.

PER SERVING

Calories: 205 | Fat: 15.5g | Fiber: 4.1g | Carbs: 8g | Protein: 8.2g

Pork Rinds

Prep time: 10 minutes | Cook time: 10 minutes | Serves 3

- 6 oz pork skin
- 1 tablespoon keto tomato sauce
- 1 teaspoon olive oil

1. Chop the pork skin into the rinds and sprinkle with the sauce and olive oil.
2. Mix up well. Then preheat the air fryer to 400F.
3. Place the pork skin rinds in the air fryer basket in one layer and cook for 10 minutes.
4. Flip the rinds on another side after 5 minutes of Cook.

PER SERVING

Calories 324 | Fat 19.3g | Fiber 0.2g | Carbs 0.3g | Protein 34.8

Lettuce Wraps with Ham and Cheese
Prep Time: 5 minutes | Cook Time: 10 minutes | Serves 5

- 10 Boston lettuce leaves, washed and rinsed well
- 1 tablespoon lemon juice, freshly squeezed
- 10 tablespoons cream cheese
- 10 thin ham slices
- 1 tomato, chopped
- 1 red chili pepper, chopped

1. Drizzle lemon juice over the lettuce leaves. Spread cream cheese over the lettuce leaves. Add a ham slice on each leaf.
2. Divide chopped tomatoes between the lettuce leaves. Top with chili peppers and arrange on a nice serving platter. Bon appétit!

PER SERVING
Calories: 148 | Fat: 10.2g | Carbs: 4.2g | Protein: 10.7g | Fiber: 0.8g

Deli Turkey and Avocado Roll-Ups
Prep Time: 5 minutes | Cook Time: 10 minutes | Serves 8

- 1/2 fresh lemon, juiced
- 2 avocados, pitted, peeled and diced
- 16 slices cooked turkey breasts, deli-sliced
- Salt and black pepper, to taste
- 16 slices Swiss cheese

1. Drizzle fresh lemon juice over your avocados. Place 1-2 avocado pieces on the turkey breast slice.
2. Season with salt and black pepper to taste.
3. Add the slice of Swiss cheese; repeat with the remaining ingredients. Roll them up and arrange on a nice serving platter. Bon appétit!

PER SERVING
Calories: 332 | Fat: 23.9g | Carbs: 7g | Protein: 22.4g | Fiber: 3.6g

Chapter 7
Chicken and Poultry

Old-Fashioned Chicken Salad

Prep time: 5 minutes | Cook time: 20 minutes | Serves 4

- 2 chicken breasts, skinless and boneless
- 1/2 teaspoon salt
- 2 bay laurels
- 1 thyme sprig 1 rosemary sprig
- 4 scallions, trimmed and thinly sliced
- 1 tablespoon fresh coriander, chopped
- teaspoon Dijon mustard
- teaspoons freshly squeezed lemon juice
- 1 cup mayonnaise, preferably homemade

1. Place all ingredients for the poached chicken in a stockpot| cover with water and bring to a rolling boil.
2. Turn the heat to medium-low and let it simmer for about 15 minutes or until a meat thermometer reads 165 degrees F.
3. Let the poached chicken cool to room temperature.
4. Cut into strips and transfer to a nice salad bowl.
5. Toss the poached chicken with the salad ingredients| serve well chilled and enjoy!

PER SERVING

Calories: 536 | Fat: 49g | Fiber: 0.5g | Carbohydrates: 3.1g | Protein: 19g

Cinnamon Chicken Wings

Prep time: 5 minutes | Cook time: 30 minutes | Serves 4

- 1 tablespoon olive oil
- 2 pounds of chicken wings
- 1 teaspoon ground cinnamon
- ½ teaspoon apple cider vinegar

1. Sprinkle the chicken wings with ground cinnamon and apple cider vinegar.
2. Then sprinkle the chicken ings with olive oil and put it in the air fryer.
3. Cook the meal at 375F for 30 minutes.
4. Flip the chicken wings from time to time to avoid burning.

PER SERVING

Calories 462 | Fat 20.3g | Fiber 0.3g | Carbs 0.5g | Protein 65.6

Marinara Chicken Wings

Prep Time: 10 minutes | **Cook Time:** 30 minutes | **Serves** 5

- 3-pounds chicken wings
- ¼ cup marinara sauce
- 1 tablespoon coconut oil, melted

1. Mix marinara sauce with coconut oil.
2. Then put the chicken wings in the air fryer basket and add marinara sauce mixture.
3. Cook the meal at 360F for 30 minutes.

PER SERVING

Calories: 551 | Fat: 23.2g | Fiber: 0.3g | Carbs: 1.7g | Protein: 79g

Capocollo-Wrapped Chicken

Prep time: 5 minutes | **Cook time:** 35 minutes | **Serves** 5

- 2 pounds chicken drumsticks, skinless and boneless
- 1 garlic clove, peeled and halved
- 1/2 teaspoon smoked paprika
- Coarse sea salt and ground black pepper, to taste
- 10 thin slices of capocollo

1. Using a sharp kitchen knife, butterfly cut the chicken drumsticks in half.
2. Lay each chicken drumstick flat on a cutting board and rub garlic halves over the surface of chicken drumsticks. Season with paprika, salt, and black pepper.
3. Lay a slice of capocollo on each piece, pressing lightly. Roll them up and secure with toothpicks.
4. Bake in the preheated oven at 420 degrees F for about 15 minutes until the edges of the chicken begin to brown.
5. Turn over and bake for a further 15 to 20 minutes. Bon appétit!

PER SERVING

Calories: 485 | Fat: 33.8g | Fiber: 1g | Carbohydrates: 3.6g | Protein: 39.2g

Chicken Quesadilla Melt
Prep Time: 15 minutes | Cook Time: 10 minutes | Serves 4

- 2 keto tortillas
- 9 oz chicken fillet, cooked, shredded
- 1 jalapeno pepper, sliced
- 3 oz Parmesan, grated
- 1 teaspoon dried dill

1. In the mixing bowl, mix shredded chicken with jalapeno pepper, Parmesan, and dried dill.
2. Then spread the mixture over the tortillas and fold them.
3. Put the tortillas in the air fryer basket and cook at 390F for 5 minutes per side.

PER SERVING
Calories: 532 | Fat: 26.6g | Fiber: 4.3g | Carbs: 10.2g | Protein: 62.8g

Sweet Chicken Wings
Prep time: 10 minutes | Cook time: 16 minutes | Serves 4

- 1-pound chicken wings
- 1 tablespoon taco seasonings
- 1 tablespoon Erythritol
- 1 tablespoon coconut oil, melted

1. Mix chicken wings with taco seasonings, Erythritol, and coconut oil.
2. Put the chicken wings in the air fryer basket and cook them at 380F for 16 minutes.

PER SERVING
Calories: 250 | Fat: 11.8g | Fiber: 0g | Carbohydrates: 3.8g | Protein: 33.1g

Garlic Duck Skin

Prep time: 5 minutes | Cook time: 6 minutes | Serves 6

- 10 oz duck skin
- 1 teaspoon avocado oil
- 1 teaspoon garlic powder

1. Mix duck skin with avocado oil and garlic powder.
2. Put it in the air fryer basket and cook for 3 minutes per side at 400F.

PER SERVING

Calories 196 | Fat 18.9g | Fiber 0.1g | Carbs 0.4g | Protein 5.6

Paprika Duck

Prep Time: 5 minutes | Cook Time: 28 minutes | Serves 6

- 10 oz duck skin
- 1 teaspoon sunflower oil
- ½ teaspoon salt
- ½ teaspoon ground paprika

1. Preheat the air fryer to 375F. Then sprinkle the duck skin with sunflower oil, salt, and ground paprika.
2. Put the duck skin in the air fryer and cook it for 18 minutes. Then flip it on another side and cook for 10 minutes more or until it is crunchy from both sides.

PER SERVING

Calories: 265 | Fat: 23.9g | Fiber: 0.1g | Carbs: 0.1g | Protein: 11.6g

Lemon Chicken Tenders

Prep Time: 5 minutes | **Cook Time:** 20 minutes | **Serves 4**

- 2-pounds chicken tenders
- 1 teaspoon lemon zest, grated
- 2 tablespoons lemon juice
- 1 tablespoon avocado oil

1. Mix avocado oil with lemon juice and lemon zest.
2. Then mix chicken tenders with lemon mixture and put in the air fryer.
3. Cook the chicken tenders at 365F for 10 minutes per side.

PER SERVING

Calories: 438 | Fat: 17.3g | Fiber: 0.2g | Carbs: 0.5g | Protein: 65.7g

Tarragon Chicken Thighs

Prep Time: 5 minutes | **Cook Time:** 30 minutes | **Serves 4**

- 2 pounds chicken thighs
- 1 tablespoon dried tarragon
- 1 tablespoon avocado oil
- ½ teaspoon salt

1. Mix chicken thighs with dried tarragon, avocado oil, and salt.
2. Put the chicken thighs in the air fryer basket and cook for 15 minutes per side at 360F.

PER SERVING

Calories: 437 | Fat: 17.3g | Fiber: 0.2g | Carbs: 0.4g | Protein: 65.8g

Pepper Cutlets
Prep time: 10 minutes | Cook time: 16 minutes | Serves 4

- 2-pounds chicken fillet
- 1 teaspoon ground black pepper
- 1 teaspoon coconut oil, melted
- 1 teaspoon chili powder

1. Sprinkle the chicken fillets with ground black pepper and chili powder and put in the air fryer basket in one layer.
2. Then sprinkle the chicken with coconut oil and cool at 380F for 8 minutes per side.

PER SERVING

Calories 444 | Fat 18.1g | Fiber 0.4g | Carbs 0.7g | Protein 65.8

Chicken Wrapped in Bacon
Prep Time: 5 minutes | Cook Time: 15 minutes | Serves 6

- 6 slices of bacon
- 1 small chicken breast
- 1 tablespoon garlic, minced
- Soft cheese

1. Chop up chicken breast into bite-sized pieces. Lay out bacon slices and spread cheese on top. Place chicken on top of cheese and roll up. Secure with a cocktail stick.
2. Place wrapped chicken pieces in air fryer and cooked for 15-minutes at 350°Fahrenheit.

PER SERVING

Calories: 296 | Total Fat: 11.8g | Carbs: 8.7g | Protein: 15.2g

Coconut Chicken Tenders

Prep time: 5 minutes | Cook time: 20 minutes | Serves 4

- 2-pounds chicken breast, skinless, boneless
- ½ cup coconut shred
- 2 eggs, beaten
- 1 teaspoon Italian seasonings

1. Cut the chicken into tenders and sprinkle with Italian seasonings.
2. Then dip the chicken tenders in the eggs and coat in the coconut shred.
3. Put the chicken tenders in the air fryer basket and cook at 370F for 10 minutes per side.

PER SERVING

Calories 394 | Fat 18.2g | Fiber 2g | Carbs 4.3g | Protein 50.9

Ginger Drumsticks

Prep time: 5 minutes | Cook time: 20 minutes | Serves 4

- 1 teaspoon ground ginger
- ½ teaspoon ground cinnamon
- 1 tablespoon olive oil
- ½ teaspoon onion powder
- 2-pounds chicken drumsticks

1. Mix the chicken drumsticks with onion powder, olive oil, ground cinnamon, and ground ginger.
2. Put them in the air fryer basket and cook at 380F for 20 minutes.

PER SERVING

Calories: 417 | Fat: 16.5g | Fiber: 0.2g | Carbohydrates: 0.8g | Protein: 62.5g

Almond Coconut Chicken Tenders

Prep Time: 5 minutes | Cook Time: 20 minutes | Serves 4

- 4 chicken breasts, skinless, boneless and cut into tenders
- A pinch of salt and black pepper
- 1/3 cup almond flour
- 2 eggs, whisked
- 9 ounces coconut flakes

1. Season the chicken tenders with salt and pepper, dredge them in almond flour, then dip in eggs and roll in coconut flakes.
2. Put the chicken tenders in your air fryer's basket and cook at 400 degrees F for 10 minutes on each side. Divide between plates and serve with a side salad.

PER SERVING

Calories: 250 | Fat: 12g | Fiber: 4g | Carbs: 6g | Protein: 15g

Garlic Butter Roasted Chicken Drumsticks

Prep time: 10 minutes | Cook time: 50 minutes | Serves 4

- 1 stick unsalted butter, softened
- 4 cloves garlic, minced
- Sea salt and ground black pepper, to taste
- 1 tablespoon fresh thyme leaves
- 2 pounds chicken drumsticks

1. In a mixing bowl, thoroughly combine the butter, garlic, salt, black pepper, and thyme.
2. Rub this mixture all over the chicken drumsticks.
3. Lay the chicken drumsticks on a parchment-lined baking tray. Bake in the preheated oven at 390 degrees F until an instant-read thermometer reads 160 degrees F about 40 minutes.
4. Place under the preheated broiler for 1 to 2 minutes if you'd like the golden, crisp skin.
5. Bon appétit!

PER SERVING

Calories 343 | Fat 24.2g | Carbs 1.6g | Protein 28.2g | Fiber 0.2g

Chapter 8
Beef, Lamb and Pork

Beef Roll-Up
Prep time: 5 minutes | Cook time: 14 minutes | Serves 4

- 2lbs. beef flank steak
- Salt and pepper to taste
- ¾ cup baby spinach, fresh
- 3-ounces red bell peppers, roasted
- 6 slices provolone cheese
- 3 tablespoons Pesto

1. Open the steak and spread the pesto evenly over the meat.
2. Layer the cheese, roasted red peppers and spinach ¾ of the way down the meat. Roll up and secure with toothpicks. Season with sea salt and pepper.
3. Preheat air fryer to 400°Fahrenheit. Place the roll-ups in the fry basket and into the air fryer and cook it for 14-minutes. Halfway through the cook time rotate the meat.
4. When cook time is completed, allow the meat to rest for 10-minutes before cutting and serving.

PER SERVING

Calories: 282 | Total Fat: 12.3g | Carbohydrates: 9.8g | Protein: 16.3g

Beef & Potato
Prep Time: 5 minutes | Cook Time: 20 minutes | Serves 4

- 2 eggs
- 3 cups mashed potatoes
- 1 lb. ground beef
- 2 tablespoons garlic powder
- 1 cup sour cream
- Pinch of salt
- Black pepper to taste

1. Preheat your air fryer to 390°Fahrenheit. Add all the ingredients into a bowl. Place ingredients in a heat safe dish and cook for 20-minutes. Serve warm.

PER SERVING

Calories: 296 | Total Fat: 12.2g | Carbs: 11.8g | Protein: 16.3g

Mustard Beef Loin
Prep Time: 10 minutes | Cook Time: 40 minutes | Serves 7

- 4-pounds beef loin
- 2 tablespoon Dijon mustard
- 1 tablespoon olive oil
- ½ tablespoon apple cider vinegar

1. Mix mustard with olive oil and apple cider vinegar.
2. Then rub the beef loin with mustard mixture and put it in the air fryer.
3. Cook the meal at 375F for 20 minutes per side.

PER SERVING

Calories: 492 | Fat: 23.8g | Fiber: 0.2g | Carbs: 0.3g | Protein: 69.5g

Cheese Burgers
Prep Time: 5 minutes | Cook Time: 11 minutes | Serves 6

- 1 lb. ground beef
- 6 slices cheddar cheese
- Salt and pepper to taste

1. Preheat the air fryer to 350°Fahrenheit. Season ground beef with pepper and salt. Make six patties from the mixture and place them into air fryer basket. Air fry patties for 10-minutes.
2. After 10-minutes, place cheese slices over patties and cook for another minute. Serve warm.

PER SERVING

Calories: 302 | Total Fat: 12.5g | Carbs: 12.2g | Protein: 16.2g

Onion Beef Bites
Prep time: 10 minutes | Cook time: 30 minutes | Serves 4

- 2-pound beef fillet
- 1 tablespoon onion powder
- ¼ cup heavy cream
- ½ teaspoon salt
- 1 teaspoon olive oil

1. Cut the beef fillet into bites and sprinkle with onion powder and salt.
2. Then put the beef bites in the air fryer and add heavy cream.
3. Cook the beef bites at 360F for 15 minutes per side.

PER SERVING

Calories 295 | Fat 14.1g | Fiber 0.1g | Carbs 5.7g | Protein 36.8

Mississippi Pork Butt Roast
Prep time: 10 minutes | Cook time: 6 hours | Serves 7

- 1 tablespoon ranch dressing mix
- 1½ pound (680 g) pork butt roast, chopped
- 1 cup butter
- 1 chili pepper, chopped
- ½ cup water

1. Put all ingredients in the instant pot.
2. Close the instant pot and cook the meal for 6 hours on Low Pressure.
3. When the time is over, shred the meat gently and transfer in the serving plate.

PER SERVING
Calories: 414 | Fat: 38g | Protein: 17g | Carbs: 0g | Net Carbs: 0g | Fiber: 0g

Garlic Butter Italian Sausages
Prep time: 15 minutes | Cook time: 20 minutes | Serves 4

- 1 teaspoon garlic powder
- 1 cup water
- 1 teaspoon butter
- 12 ounces (340 g) Italian sausages, chopped
- ½ teaspoons Italian seasoning

1. Sprinkle the chopped Italian sausages with Italian seasoning and garlic powder and place in the instant pot.
2. Add butter and cook the sausages on Sauté mode for 10 minutes. Stir them from time to time with the help of the spatula.
3. Then add water and close the lid.
4. Cook the sausages on Manual mode (High Pressure) for 10 minutes.
5. Allow the natural pressure release for 10 minutes more.

PER SERVING
Calories: 307 | fat: 28g | protein: 12g | carbs: 1g | net carbs: 1g | fiber: 0g

Air-Fried Rib Eye Steak
Prep time: 5 minutes | Cook time: 14 minutes | Serves 4

- 2 lbs. ribeye steak
- Salt and pepper to taste
- 1 tablespoon olive oil
- 2 tablespoons of steak rub

1. Preheat your air fryer to 390°Fahrenheit.
2. Rub the steak with seasoning, salt, pepper on both sides.
3. Sprinkle the basket with olive oil and place the steak inside of it.
4. Cook steak for seven minutes on one side then flip it over and cook on the other side for an additional seven minutes. Serve warm.

PER SERVING
Calories: 278 | Total Fat: 12.6g | Carbohydrates: 10.4g | Protein: 16.7g

Basil Pork
Prep Time: 5 minutes | Cook Time: 25 minutes | Serves 4

- 4 pork chops
- A pinch of salt and black pepper
- 2 teaspoons basil, dried
- 2 tablespoons olive oil
- ½ teaspoon chili powder

1. In a pan that fits your air fryer, mix all the ingredients, toss, introduce in the fryer and cook at 400 degrees F for 25 minutes.
2. Divide everything between plates and serve.

PER SERVING
Calories: 274 | Fat: 13g | Fiber: 4g | Carbs: 6g | Protein: 18g

Mustard Pork
Prep time: 5 minutes | Cook time: 30 minutes | Serves 4

- 1 pound pork tenderloin, trimmed
- A pinch of salt and black pepper
- 2 tablespoons olive oil
- 3 tablespoons mustard
- 2 tablespoons balsamic vinegar

1. In a bowl, mix the pork tenderloin with the rest of the ingredients and rub well.
2. Put the roast in your air fryer's basket and cook at 380 degrees F for 30 minutes.
3. Slice the roast, divide between plates and serve.

PER SERVING
Calories 274 | Fat 13g | Fiber 4g | Carbs 7g | Protein 22

Tomato Rib Eye Steaks
Prep Time: 10 minutes | Cook Time: 24 minutes | Serves 4

- 3-pound rib-eye steak
- 1 tablespoon keto tomato paste
- 1 tablespoon avocado oil
- 1 teaspoon salt
- 1 teaspoon cayenne pepper

1. In the shallow bowl, mix tomato paste with avocado oil, salt, and cayenne pepper.
2. Then run the beef with tomato mixture and put it in the air fryer.
3. Cook the meal at 380F for 12 minutes per side.

PER SERVING

Calories: 943 | Fat: 75.8g | Fiber: 0.4g | Carbs: 1.2g | Protein: 60.5g

Turmeric Pork Loin
Prep time: 10 minutes | Cook time: 22 minutes | Serves 4

- 1 pound (454 g) pork loin
- 1 teaspoon ground turmeric
- 1 teaspoon coconut oil
- ½ teaspoons salt
- ½ cup organic almond milk

1. Cut the pork loin into the strips and sprinkle with salt and ground turmeric.
2. Heat up the coconut oil on Sauté mode for 1 minute and add pork strips.
3. Sauté them for 6 minutes. Stir the meat from time to time.
4. After this, add almond milk and close the lid.
5. Sauté the pork for 15 minutes.

PER SERVING

Calories: 226 | fat: 11g | protein: 30g | carbs: 2g | net carbs: 2g | fiber: 0g

BBQ Beef
Prep time: 15 minutes | Cook time: 15 minutes | Serves 4

- 4 beef steaks
- 1 cup keto BBQ sauce
- 1 tablespoon olive oil

1. Mix olive oil with BBQ sauce.
2. Then mix beef steaks with sauce mixture and put in the air fryer.
3. Cook the beef at 400F for 15 minutes.

PER SERVING

Calories: 603 | Fat: 25.3g | Fiber: 0.4g | Carbs: 2.7g | Protein: 66.2

Vinegar Pork Chops
Prep Time: 10 minutes | Cook Time: 20 minutes | Serves 4

- 4 pork chops
- ¼ cup apple cider vinegar
- 1 teaspoon ground black pepper
- 1 teaspoon olive oil

1. Mix apple cider vinegar with olive oil and ground black pepper.
2. Then mix pork chops with apple cider vinegar mixture.
3. Put the meat in the air fryer and cook it at 375F for 10 minutes per side.

PER SERVING

Calories: 271 | Fat: 21.1g | Fiber: 0.1g | Carbs: 0.5g | Protein: 18g

Pork and Peppers Mix
Prep time: 5 minutes | Cook time: 25 minutes | Serves 4

- 1 pound pork tenderloin, sliced
- ¼ cup cilantro, chopped
- ½ teaspoon garlic powder
- 1 tablespoon olive oil
- 1 green bell pepper, julienned
- ½ teaspoon chili powder
- ½ teaspoon cumin, ground

1. Heat up a pan that fits the air fryer with the oil over medium heat, add the pork and brown for 5 minutes.
2. Add the rest of the ingredients, toss, put the pan in the air fryer and cook at 400 degrees F for 20 minutes.
3. Divide between plates and serve.

PER SERVING

Calories: 284 | Fat: 13g | Fiber: 4g | Carbohydrates: 6g | Protein: 17g

Chapter 9
Fish and Seafood

Almond Catfish

Prep time: 10 minutes | Cook time: 12 minutes | Serves 4

- 2-pound catfish fillet
- ½ cup almond flour
- 2 eggs, beaten
- 1 teaspoon salt
- 1 teaspoon avocado oil

1. Sprinkle the catfish fillet with salt and dip in the eggs.
2. Then coat the fish in the almond flour and put in the air fryer basket. Sprinkle the fish with avocado oil.
3. Cook the fish for 6 minutes per side at 380F.

PER SERVING

Calories: 423 | Fat: 26.2g | Fiber: 1.6g | Carbohydrates: 3.2g | Protein: 41.1g

Breaded Fish

Prep time: 5 minutes | Cook time: 12 minutes | Serves 4

- 4 fish fillets
- 1 egg
- 5-ounces breadcrumbs
- 4 tablespoons olive oil

1. Preheat your air fryer to 350°Fahrenheit.
2. In a bowl mix oil and breadcrumbs. Whisk egg. Gently dip the fish into egg and then into crumb mixture.
3. Put into air fryer and cook for 12-minutes.

PER SERVING

Calories: 302 | Total Fat: 10.4g | Carbohydrates: 8.9g | Protein: 14.6g

Steamed Halibut with Thyme and Sesame

Prep time: 25 minutes | Cook time: 15 minutes | Serves 4

- 8 oz. halibut, cut into 2 portions
- 1 tbsp. lemon juice, freshly squeezed
- 1 tsp. dried thyme leaves
- 1 tbsp. sesame seeds, toasted
- Salt and pepper to taste

1. Place a trivet in a large saucepan and pour a cup or two of water into the pan. Bring it to a boil.
2. Place halibut in a heatproof dish that fits inside a saucepan. Season with lemon juice, salt, and pepper. Sprinkle with dried thyme leaves and sesame seeds.
3. Seal dish with foil. Place the dish on the trivet inside the saucepan. Cover and steam for 15 minutes.
4. Serve and enjoy.

PER SERVING

Calories: 245 | Fat: 17.6g | Carbs: 4.1g | Protein: 17.4g

Blackened Snapper

Prep Time: 5 minutes | Cook Time: 7 minutes | Serves 4

- 4 (6-ounce) snapper or other white fish fillets
- ½ teaspoon kosher salt
- ¼ cup Blackening Seasoning
- 2 tablespoons butter

1. Season the fish fillets with the salt, then coat them with the blackening seasoning on all sides.
2. Heat the butter in a medium-sized nonstick skillet over high heat until bubbling. Add the fish and cook for 2 to 3 minutes per side, until it becomes opaque and flakes easily. Remove from the pan and serve immediately.

PER SERVING

Calories: 241 | Fat: 9g | Protein: 36g | Carbs: 4g | Fiber: 2g

Cajun-Seasoned Lemon Salmon

Prep Time: 2 minutes | Cook Time: 7 minutes | Serves 1

- 1 salmon fillet
- 1 teaspoon Cajun seasoning
- 1 teaspoon liquid stevia
- ½ lemon, juiced

1. Preheat your air fryer to 350°Fahrenheit. Combine lemon juice and liquid stevia and coat salmon with this mixture. Sprinkle Cajun seasoning all over salmon. Place salmon on parchment paper in air fryer and cook for 7-minutes.
2. Serve with lemon wedges.

PER SERVING

Calories: 287 | Total Fat: 9.3g | Carbs: 8.4g | Protein: 15.3g

Shrimp Salad

Prep Time: 5 minutes | Cook Time: 5 minutes | Serves 3

- 2 large avocados, cut in half and pitted (leave skin on)
- 1 cup extra-small (100–150 count per pound) peeled, deveined, and cooked shrimp

1. In a medium bowl, whisk together all Dressing ingredients.
2. Enlarge the holes left by the pits in the avocados by scooping out some avocado using a spoon. Leave at least a ¼" ring of avocado flesh along the outer edge of the avocados.
3. Combine scooped-out avocado, shrimp, and celery with the Dressing. Stir to mix.
4. Evenly divide shrimp mixture into the holes in each avocado half.
5. Cover with plastic wrap and refrigerate until ready to serve. Serve chilled.

PER SERVING

Calories: 257 | Fat: 20g | Carbs: 1.1g | Protein: 3.3g

Steamed Dill Cappers Flounder
Prep Time: 5 minutes | Cook Time: 15 minutes | Serves 4

- 4 flounder fillets
- 1 tbsp. chopped fresh dill
- 2 tbsp. capers, chopped
- 4 lemon wedges
- 6 tbsp olive oil
- Salt and pepper to taste

1. Place a trivet in a large saucepan and pour a cup or two of water into the pan. Bring to a boil.
2. Place flounder in a heatproof dish that fits inside a saucepan. Season snapper with pepper and salt. Drizzle with olive oil on all sides. Sprinkle dill and capers on top of the filet.
3. Seal dish with foil. Place the dish on the trivet inside the saucepan. Cover and steam for 15 minutes.
4. Serve and enjoy with lemon wedges.

PER SERVING

Calories: 446| Fat: 35.8g| Carbs: 8.5g| Protein: 20.2g

Spicy Shrimp-Stuffed Avocados
Prep Time: 5 minutes, plus 10 minutes to chill| Cook Time: 5 minutes | Serves 4

- 1 pound large shrimp, peeled, deveined, and cooked (tails removed)
- ⅓ cup sugar-free mayonnaise
- 2 tablespoons Sriracha sauce
- 1 teaspoon chopped fresh cilantro, plus more for garnish if desired
- 1 teaspoon lime juice
- 2 large ripe Hass avocados

1. Chop the shrimp into bite-sized pieces and place in a medium-sized bowl.
2. Add the mayonnaise, Sriracha, cilantro, and lime juice. Mix until well combined. Place in the refrigerator to chill for 10 minutes.
3. Just before serving, cut the avocados in half and remove the pits. Spoon ½ cup of the spicy shrimp mixture into each avocado half. Serve immediately, garnished with extra cilantro, if desired. If not consuming it right away, store the spicy shrimp mixture in the refrigerator for up to 5 days.

PER SERVING

Calories: 334 | Fat: 29g | Protein: 15g | Carbs: 8g | Fiber: 5g

Shrimp Caprese Salad
Prep Time: 12 minutes, plus 30 minutes to chill| Cook Time: 5 minutes | Serves 4

- 1 pound large shrimp, peeled, deveined, and cooked
- 1 cup halved cherry tomatoes
- 4 ounces fresh mozzarella, cut into 1-inch cubes
- 2 tablespoons chopped fresh basil, plus more for garnish if desired
- 1 batch Creamy Basil-Parmesan Vinaigrette

1. Cut the shrimp in half lengthwise and place in a medium-sized salad bowl.
2. Add the tomatoes, mozzarella, and basil to the bowl. Pour the vinaigrette over the salad ingredients and toss to coat.
3. For best flavor, chill for 30 minutes before serving. Garnish the salad with additional chopped basil, if desired.

PER SERVING

Calories: 371 | Fat: 27g | Protein: 30g | Carbs: 3g | Fiber: 1g

Classic Rosemary Shrimps
Prep Time: 5 minutes | Cook Time: 10 minutes | Serves 4

- 5 tablespoons butter
- ½ cup lemon juice, freshly squeezed
- 1 ½ lb. shrimps, peeled and deveined
- ¼ cup coconut aminos
- 1 tsp rosemary
- Pepper to taste

1. Place all ingredients in a large pan on a high fire.
2. Boil for 8 minutes or until shrimps are pink.
3. Serve and enjoy.

PER SERVING

Calories: 314| Fat: 17.8g| Carbs: 3.6g| Protein: 35.7g

Lime Cod
Prep Time: 5 minutes | Cook Time: 14 minutes | Serves 4

- 4 cod fillets, boneless
- 1 tablespoon olive oil
- Salt and black pepper to the taste
- 2 teaspoons sweet paprika
- Juice of 1 lime

1. In a bowl, mix all the ingredients, transfer the fish to your air fryer's basket and cook 350 degrees F for 7 minutes on each side.
2. Divide the fish between plates and serve with a side salad.

PER SERVING

Calories: 240 | Fat: 14g | Fiber: 2g | Carbs: 4g | Protein: 16g

Coco Ginger Curry Cod
Prep Time: 15 minutes | Cook Time: 20 minutes | Serves 4

- 4 cod fillets
- 1½ cups coconut milk, freshly squeezed if possible
- 2 tsp. grated ginger
- 2 tsp. curry powder
- 1 sprig cilantro, chopped
- Salt and pepper to taste

1. Add all ingredients in a nonstick saucepan. Cover and cook for 10 minutes on a high fire.
2. Lower fire to a simmer and simmer for 7 minutes.
3. Season with pepper and salt.
4. Serve and enjoy.

NUTRITION FACTS PER SERVING

Calories: 290| Fat: 22 g| Carbs: 5.6g| Protein: 19.6g

Mustard Cod
Prep Time: 10 minutes | Cook Time: 14 minutes | Serves 4

- 1 cup parmesan, grated
- 4 cod fillets, boneless
- Salt and black pepper to the taste
- 1 tablespoon mustard

1. In a bowl, mix the parmesan with salt, pepper and the mustard and stir. Spread this over the cod, arrange the fish in the air fryer's basket and cook at 370 degrees F for 7 minutes on each side.
2. Divide between plates and serve with a side salad.

PER SERVING

Calories: 270 | Fat: 14g | Fiber: 3g | Carbs: 5g | Protein: 12g

Appendix 1 Measurement Conversion Chart

Volume Equivalents (Dry)	
US STANDARD	METRIC (APPROXIMATE)
1/8 teaspoon	0.5 mL
1/4 teaspoon	1 mL
1/2 teaspoon	2 mL
3/4 teaspoon	4 mL
1 teaspoon	5 mL
1 tablespoon	15 mL
1/4 cup	59 mL
1/2 cup	118 mL
3/4 cup	177 mL
1 cup	235 mL
2 cups	475 mL
3 cups	700 mL
4 cups	1 L

Volume Equivalents (Liquid)		
US STANDARD	US STANDARD (OUNCES)	METRIC (APPROXIMATE)
2 tablespoons	1 fl.oz.	30 mL
1/4 cup	2 fl.oz.	60 mL
1/2 cup	4 fl.oz.	120 mL
1 cup	8 fl.oz.	240 mL
1 1/2 cup	12 fl.oz.	355 mL
2 cups or 1 pint	16 fl.oz.	475 mL
4 cups or 1 quart	32 fl.oz.	1 L
1 gallon	128 fl.oz.	4 L

Temperatures Equivalents	
FAHRENHEIT(F)	CELSIUS(C) APPROXIMATE)
225 °F	107 °C
250 °F	120 ° °C
275 °F	135 °C
300 °F	150 °C
325 °F	160 °C
350 °F	180 °C
375 °F	190 °C
400 °F	205 °C
425 °F	220 °C
450 °F	235 °C
475 °F	245 °C
500 °F	260 °C

Weight Equivalents	
US STANDARD	METRIC (APPROXIMATE)
1 ounce	28 g
2 ounces	57 g
5 ounces	142 g
10 ounces	284 g
15 ounces	425 g
16 ounces (1 pound)	455 g
1.5 pounds	680 g
2 pounds	907 g

Appendix 2 The Dirty Dozen and Clean Fifteen

The Environmental Working Group (EWG) is a nonprofit, nonpartisan organization dedicated to protecting human health and the environment Its mission is to empower people to live healthier lives in a healthier environment. This organization publishes an annual list of the twelve kinds of produce, in sequence, that have the highest amount of pesticide residue-the Dirty Dozen-as well as a list of the fifteen kinds of produce that have the least amount of pesticide residue-the Clean Fifteen.

THE DIRTY DOZEN	
The 2016 Dirty Dozen includes the following produce. These are considered among the year's most important produce to buy organic:	
Strawberries	Spinach
Apples	Tomatoes
Nectarines	Bell peppers
Peaches	Cherry tomatoes
Celery	Cucumbers
Grapes	Kale/collard greens
Cherries	Hot peppers
The Dirty Dozen list contains two additional itemskale/collard greens and hot peppers-because they tend to contain trace levels of highly hazardous pesticides.	

THE CLEAN FIFTEEN	
The least critical to buy organically are the Clean Fifteen list. The following are on the 2016 list:	
Avocados	Papayas
Corn	Kiw
Pineapples	Eggplant
Cabbage	Honeydew
Sweet peas	Grapefruit
Onions	Cantaloupe
Asparagus	Cauliflower
Mangos	
Some of the sweet corn sold in the United States are made from genetically engineered (GE) seedstock. Buy organic varieties of these crops to avoid GE produce.	

Appendix 3 Index

A

all-purpose flour 50, 53
allspice 15
almond 5, 14
ancho chile 10
ancho chile powder 5
apple 9
apple cider vinegar 9
arugula 51
avocado 11

B

bacon 52
balsamic vinegar 7, 12, 52
basil 5, 8, 11, 13
beet 52
bell pepper 50, 51, 53
black beans 50, 51
broccoli 51, 52, 53
buns 52
butter 50

C

canola oil 50, 51, 52
carrot 52, 53
cauliflower 5, 52
cayenne 5, 52
cayenne pepper 52
Cheddar cheese 52
chicken 6
chili powder 50, 51
chipanle pepper 50
chives 5, 6, 52
cinnamon 15
coconut 6
Colby Jack cheese 51
coriander 52
corn 50, 51
corn kernels 50
cumin 5, 10, 15, 50, 51, 52

D

diced panatoes 50
Dijon mustard 7, 12, 13, 51
dry onion powder 52

E

egg 14, 50, 53
enchilada sauce 51

F

fennel seed 53
flour 50, 53
fresh chives 5, 6, 52
fresh cilantro 52
fresh cilantro leaves 52
fresh dill 5
fresh parsley 6, 52
fresh parsley leaves 52

G

garlic 5, 9, 10, 11, 13, 14, 50, 51, 52, 53
garlic powder 8, 9, 52, 53

H

half-and-half 50
hemp seeds 8
honey 9, 51

I

instant rice 51

K

kale 14
kale leaves 14
ketchup 53
kosher salt 5, 10, 15

L

lemon 5, 6, 14, 51, 53
lemon juice 6, 8, 11, 13, 14, 51
lime 9, 12
lime juice 9, 12
lime zest 9, 12

M

maple syrup 7, 12, 53
Marinara Sauce 5
micro greens 52
milk 5, 50
mixed berries 12
Mozzarella 50, 53
Mozzarella cheese 50, 53
mushroom 51, 52
mustard 51, 53
mustard powder 53

N

nutritional yeast 5

O

olive oil 5, 12, 13, 14, 50, 51, 52, 53
onion 5, 50, 51
onion powder 8
oregano 5, 8, 10, 50

P

panatoes 50, 52
paprika 5, 15, 52
Parmesan cheese 51, 53
parsley 6, 52
pesto 52
pink Himalayan salt 5, 7, 8, 11
pizza dough 50, 53
pizza sauce 50
plain coconut yogurt 6
plain Greek yogurt 5
porcini powder 53
potato 53

R

Ranch dressing 52
raw honey 9, 12, 13
red pepper flakes 5, 8, 14, 15, 51, 53
ricotta cheese 53

S

saffron 52
Serrano pepper 53
sugar 10
summer squash 51

T

tahini 5, 8, 9, 11
thyme 50
toasted almonds 14
tomato 5, 50, 52, 53
turmeric 15

U

unsalted butter 50
unsweetened almond milk 5

V

vegetable broth 50
vegetable stock 51

W

white wine 8, 11
wine vinegar 8, 10, 11

Y

yogurt 5, 6

Z

zucchini 50, 51, 52, 53

GLORIA R. REED

Printed in Great Britain
by Amazon